W.L. ANDRIES

JOURNEY OF DISCOVERY
A BOOK OF POEMS

Word for Word
Publishing Co., Inc.
Brooklyn, NY

ALL RIGHTS RESERVED. No part of this publication may be used or reproduced in whole or in part, or transmitted in any form or by any means electronic, mechanical, photocopying, or otherwise without written permission of the copyright holder.

For permission to use copyrighted material, grateful acknowledgment is made to the copyright holder. For information, address the publisher.

Journey of Discovery: *A Book of Poems*
Copyright © 2005 by The Rev. Dr. William Lloyd Andries

Cover Designed by: MeloDesignz

Word For Word Publishing Co., Inc.
Brooklyn, New York
800-601-WORD (9673)

Library of Congress Cataloging-in-Publication Data:
2005928897
ISBN: 1-889732-23-0

Printed in the United States of America

Inspirational Poetry

Contents

Dedication . . . . *ix*
Acknowledgments . . . . *x*
Foreword . . . . *xiii*
The Poet's Message . . . . *xv*

AWARENESS
The Sunflower 20
Freedom 21
Discovery of Self 22

THE BIRTH OF IMAGINATION
Guyana 24
Land of Many Waters 25
The Golden Arrowhead 27
Mount Roraima 28
Guyanese Amerindians Speak 29
The Lure of Guyana's Offsprings 31
The Amazon River 33
Kaieteur Falls 34

THE ELEMENTS OF NATURE
I Heard the Kiskadee Sing 36
Aunt Madeline 37
Youth 38
Bullying 39
Hummingbird 40
The Peacock 41
Thunder, Lightning and Rain 42

THE MIND AND SPIRIT EMBRACE EACH OTHER

I Dreamt I Went to Heaven 44
The Rose 45
Treasure Chests 46
The Cross on the Wall 47
God Strengthens Marriage 48
Nine-Eleven 49
A Mother's Prayer 50
God Answers Prayers 51
Preachers Are Humans 52
A Chosen Vessel 53

ASSESSING LIFE

Diamonds Are Forever 56
A Happy Occasion 57
Beautiful Memories 58
Hasta Luego 59
Death Be Not Unkind 60

LIVING AND LOVING

Yankees Collapse 62
The Dentist's Chair 63
Fashion 65
The Adorable Diva 66
Enduring Beauty 67
A Love That Dares Not Whisper its Name ... 69
A World Awaits Your Skill 70
A Time of Maturation 71

ENVISIONING HOPE

Tsunami 74
Arise, Grenada 75
The Ultimate Blessing 77
Cold and Exposed 78
Good Friday 79
Brooklyn 81
The Saffron Gates of Central Park 82
Image 83
A Second Chance 84
An Old Woman of East Indian Birth 85
I Remember You, Ma 86
God Will Provide 87

Dedication

To my beloved daughter, Yma Ava Michelle Andries, for her ever-present love and in memory of my deceased wife, Barbara Taljit-Andries, whose encouraging spirit is constantly with me.

To Dr. Juliet Emanuel-George for her constant guidance throughout this process.

Finally, to all Guyanese Amerindians, the voices of whom are seldom heard.

Acknowledgments

Along the *Journey of Discovery* there have been many individuals who have encouraged me to express my thoughts in this book of poetry. They fall into various categories: relatives, friends, well-wishers, proofreaders, editors and authors. Heartfelt thanks to all of them for their advice, patience and expertise.

Yma Andries, Dorrit Bodden, V. Peter Branch, Elaine DeSantos, Olney Edwards, Dr. Juliet Emanuel-George, Claire Goring, The Rev. Dr. William Guthrie, Winston Gurley, Joyce P. Nightingale-Holder, Christopher and Sandra Hunte, The Rev. Dr. Evelyn R. John, Gloria John, Ronald and Edna Loncke, Clarence Massiah, Dr. Lorna McBarnette, Dr. V. Michael McKenzie, Yvette Richards, Donna Rossan, Norma Sainsbury, Harold Small, Ponsford Smith, Dr. Moses Telford, Dr. Marguerite Thompson, The Rev. Canon Howard K. Williams and Mrs. Shuk Fong Lee whose artwork inspired the cover.

Foreword

At least once in every lifetime the creative urge rises to the top and issues forth in great works of art, painting and sculpture, dance and music, prose and poetry. Such is this seminal book of poems from the hands and heart of a master craftsman, The Rev. Dr. William Lloyd Andries, who plumbs the depths of suffering and joy and comes up with a remarkable book of poetry that will whet your appetite and leave you asking for more.

From the crucible of his own experience, Dr. Andries skillfully assembles an anthology of poems that spans the spectrum of human emotions and gives voice to the aspect of being and longing which only the poet can describe. He reaches both the depths of agony and heights of ecstasy as he brings to birth images and ideas with which you can readily identify and which you can easily assimilate.

A man of uncanny wisdom and innate ability, Dr. Andries is a retired Episcopalian Priest who hails from Guyana in South America, "the Land of Many Waters." In more ways than one, his book of poetry reflects a background where themes of love and beauty, peace and contentment, happiness and despair, are delicately intertwined like the waters of this South American land from which he comes.

He writes with pathos and poignancy about the issues and events that have molded his entire life, not the least of which was spent as a Chaplain to the Armed Forces, a notable Scholar and successful

Teacher, and an avid connoisseur of the Performing Arts. These experiences, coupled with his rich Amerindian ancestry, have formed a poet whose remarkable skill and artistry can be seen in this outstanding collection of verse.

As a personal friend and confidant, I have the distinct privilege and utmost pleasure in commending this work of my mentor and teacher to a much wider audience for he kindles the poetic imagination and stirs the sleeping soul. Here is a feast both for the heart and the mind. You will not regret sitting down with this book in the comfort of your home for hours of contemplative pleasure. It is a work of art but it is also "a thing of beauty," and beauty as the poet knows is a joy forever because such beautiful thoughts are turned into such exquisite words.

—William Guthrie
West Orange, NJ
December 7, 2004

Poet's Message

This volume of poems contains a variety of moods, situations and places. The pendulum swings from childhood when my romance with nature began, to adulthood when I was able to peep through the keyhole of history. It encompasses sadness, gaiety and various shades of expressions and emotions along the *Journey of Discovery*.

"The Sunflower," acting as a catalyst, jolted my memory and thus evolved nostalgia. The nationalistic poems weave a patchwork of ethnicity and act as a backdrop to showcase the indigenous people of Guyana. The poems, "I heard the Kiskadee Sing," about my mother, and "Beautiful Memories," about my wife, are deeply personal as was "Nine-Eleven." The religious poems and that of Brooklyn, my present place of abode, helped me to better understand and appreciate people and places.

A poet enjoys the dual roles of visionary and pragmatist who interprets life to others.

Life is a kaleidoscope of intricate patterns and shades of colors waiting to be experienced and expressed. Live it!

JOURNEY OF DISCOVERY
A BOOK OF POEMS

AWARENESS

Journey of Discovery

The Sunflower

The sunflower never appealed to me.
It always seemed so big for all to see.
Yet no flower wears a happier smile
And beckons to you from quarter of a mile.

As the name so aptly shows,
It greets the sun wherever it goes.
In fact, it turns its head to say hello
And flashes a smile from a haze of yellow.

The essence of its being became rather clear
When I received a sunflower birthday card this year.
Followed by a phone call extolling my gifts.
Exemplified by a single sunflower, the way it shifts.

Now I see the sunflower from a different perspective.
It greets everyone, teaching us how to live.
It is lovely and as friendly as can be.
Apparently, this is how my friends see me.

Freedom

Let freedom be
Your great Epiphany
Simply discover yourself.

Freedom begins in the heart
Which is an art
Capture the feeling.

Freedom is spiritual
And can be a ritual
Experience the thrill.

The senses, body, spirit
All transport you to a different level
A mere taste of heaven.

Freedom can prove elusive
To those who would like to know
Why there's nothing to show.

Dedicated to Yma Ava Michelle Andries, my daughter

Discovery of Self

Questionable feelings disturbed my heart,
Emitting a message of unimaginable thought
And informing me from the start
That here was a web in which I was caught.

Everything around me looked divine.
At last, life had a different meaning.
Things changed from the ridiculous to the sublime,
And each day saw me beaming.

The sleeping giant in me was awakened
And I was ready for the thrill.
No longer will I feel lost and forsaken
And think of life as a boring drill.

I began to admire colors of different hue
And saw all humans as flowers in a garden.
I asked myself, "Is this really true?"
I no longer felt I was carrying a burden.

What had really happened to me
Was the discovery of self in patterns of love,
And I was a changed individual for all to see
By accepting and counting my blessings from above.

The Birth of Imagination

Guyana

South America, great continent to me,
Covered in flora and fauna for all to see.
For centuries, adventurers had their doubt
And in pursuit of it ofttimes lost their route.

Men dreamt of El Dorado or so they say,
And hoped one day to find the golden way.
After years of twists and turns on sea
Land was spotted and they faced their destiny.

Guyana, a place of rivers, plains and mountain range
Presented itself as something strange.
Outstanding and magnificent stood the Kaieteur Falls
Echoing the sounds of mysterious calls.

Diamond, Bauxite and Lumber were soon to be found
Along with other treasures as explorers searched around.
But unimpressed were the Amerindian tribes
Sensing tremendous changes would come to their lives.

Europeans of different ethnicity
Envisioned wealth and the birth of a great city.
Unfortunately they plundered and pillaged the land,
Hoping that the natives would understand.

What they did was a cowardly deed
Destroying simple people who were in need.
Today they boast of having done good
Because the country has gained nationhood.

THE BIRTH OF IMAGINATION

Land of Many Waters (February 2005)

O Guyana, your children mourn your recent fate,
A great misfortune for sure.
As waters rushed through your gate
It proved too much to endure.

Ironically, deluge of angry waters invaded the scenic
East Coast
Claiming lands and houses along the way
And silencing anyone who ever dared to boast
As they witnessed the rising floods from day to day.

While Mahaica and Ogle residents questioned their worth,
Confused and angry homeowners pondered their fate.
Every time they gazed upon their place of birth
They tried very hard to hold on to their faith.

Torrents doused Buxton, Haslington and Enmore
Together with the coast of Good Hope,
Disregarding a biblical promise not to flood the earth
anymore.
Yet believers looked for a Rainbow of Hope.

Thus, folks knew that all was not lost
Because past experiences stood them in good stead
Reminding them to rebuild at all costs
Knowing that challenges will only cease when
you're dead.

Journey of Discovery

O Guyana, land of many waters,
You must with this crisis deal,
Because in the end what really matters
Is that your children be housed and be able to eat a good meal.

The Golden Arrowhead

Golden Arrowhead, you stand proud and majestic!
Symbol of a people, once oppressed now free.
A colorful flag embracing the elements for all to see
In the face of adversity, you remain nationalistic.

You embody the history of a great land.
There is wealth to be unearthed from its treacherous bed.
Agriculture must remain a means by which your people will be fed.
Through it all, determination and endurance go hand in hand.

As the rivers of this country show,
Tides may ebb high and low
But there is only one direction in which to go.
The Golden Arrowhead proclaims daily,
"I told you so."

Go forward Guyana and take your place.
The Golden Arrowhead points the way.
As your foreparents successfully held sway,
You too can win the race through strength and grace.

Mount Roraima

Roraima, ancestral home of Amerindian gods!
Papi fashioned this tripartite border of Guyana,
Venezuela and Brazil, so, sing alleluia.
Your daunting peak seems to touch the clouds
While your windswept plateau
Embraces flora and fauna close to your breast
Where rare birds come to make their nest.
You welcome all to your magnificent château.

Humans who dare to challenge your strength
Climb upward and onward to self-destruction
Even though they are aware of lots of obstruction.
People often go to great length
As if to question the Omniscient.
May discretion and valor be their guide
Because Mount Roraima is no place to hide.
You stand as a monument to the Omnipotent.

The Birth of Imagination

Guyanese Amerindians Speak

We are the nine tribes of Guyana free
Who have said very little before.
We dwell in the hinterland where you would
expect us to be.
Over twelve hundred years ago, our ancestors
discovered this shore.

Columbus has been mistakenly acclaimed
As the discoverer of our great domain.
The indigenous people of this land were murdered
and maimed.
Atrocities were committed by people who seemed
insane.

Things did not change with the influx of others.
Our men continued to be slaughtered
and our women raped.
Missionaries, on the other hand, preached about
being brothers
Fed up with rhetoric and lies some of our people
negated.

Diseases unknown before even in the Savannahs
Became commonplace and a curse to us all.
It was a sad day for the Arawaks, Ackawaois
and Arekunas
While the Wai Wais, Wapishanas and Warraus
sensed a great fall.

Journey of Discovery

A quiet people content with fishing and hunting
Showed great resistance against their foes.
The Caribs, Patamonas and Macushi took a beating
Cassava bread eating and casiri drinking only added to their woes

Guyana, land of many waters.
This Amerindian word pays tribute to our tribes.
A posthumous victory has been won by our ancestors
Who truly survived by giving up their lives.

Descendants from Europe, Africa, Portugal, China and India
Now make up our nation.
We will strive with them to fulfill our motto-
One People, One Nation, One Destiny.
This is our heritage and our only salvation.
Perhaps Amerindians will at last be treated with respect and dignity.

THE BIRTH OF IMAGINATION

The Lure of Guyana's Offsprings

Guyana, vast land of virgin soil,
Stands unique in shape and rich in spoil.
South America, your home of choice,
Placed you at The Northern Edge
and gave you a voice.

Venezuela, Brazil, Suriname
All act as guardians to keep you from harm.
Your Spanish, Portuguese and Dutch-speaking neighbors
Hope that one day you would repay favors.

Your triplet offsprings caused you to grow,
And so you aptly named them Demerara, Berbice and Essequibo.
Each county as they are known today
Was soon to encourage investors from far away.

Your major resources of timber, bauxite, diamonds and gold
Confirmed rumors of wealth wherever they were told.
Thus began the search into the unknown
Causing many men to wander and roam.

Thousands of individuals lost their lives
By refusing to listen to the advice of the wise.
What began as a search of wealth and fame
Soon developed into a curse and downright shame.

Journey of Discovery

The treacherous waters eagerly devoured its prey.
The Demerara, Berbice and Essequibo Rivers now
had their say,
Yet from these very riverbeds
Were unearthed gold and diamonds for European
heads.

The three offsprings of Guyana will always be givers
Because of their rich soil and flowing rivers.
Each county is special and unique.
Simply accept the challenge and go out to seek.

The Amazon River

Great Amazon of South American flow
Only your sister Nile has further to go.
Your volume of water is the greatest of any river.
You certainly know how and where to deliver.

The Amazon River, a lovely sounding name!
You have acquired notoriety and fame.
You are the matriarch of all you survey
Tributaries, land, trees, animals and everything along the way.

There's controversy about your real name,
This historical fact is no game
Whether from Greek mythology or a native American word,
It does not stop your curvaceous body from moving forward.

Beauty runs through your veins,
Enhanced at times by heavy rains.
Your bowels produce such unusual fish
As flesh-eating piranhas and the gigantic arapaima, an odd dish.

Your length and depth are really amazing.
Your width no less intriguing
Your mouth, which opens for ninety miles, is fantastic
Allowing the flow of sedimented freshwater to disappear into the salty Atlantic.

Journey of Discovery

Kaieteur Falls

Kaie, the old and wise Toshao,
Looked up to the heavens and knitted his brow.
A message was transmitted to this great Patamona,
A sacrifice was necessary to appease Makonaima.

The Patamonas and Caribs who drew imaginary walls
Would at last enjoy peace once Kaie went
over the falls.
The devastating gorge beckoned to the chief
Whose canoe steered him to a watery grave
and tribal relief.

Kaieteur Falls will always a legend be
To the many people who travel to see
A breathtaking wonder in the Potaro River
Of thunderous and cascading water of silver.

Eight hundred and twenty-two feet of water
leaping out of the sky
Caused the death of a chief and now we know
why.
Kaie and Teur combine to form a name
Because things were never to be the same.

Kaieteur Falls, what a spectacular show!
At times, it mirrors even the rainbow.
Exotic birds enjoy its radiant beauty and flow
While luxuriant plants smile as they grow

34

The Elements of Nature

Journey of Discovery

I Heard the Kiskadee Sing

I heard the Kiskadee sing
One bright and sunny day.
The plaintive notes from a feathered friend
Were to prepare me for my mother's end.

While on my way to visit my sick mother,
I stopped to play cricket with friends
Who although aware of my true mission
Encouraged me with this selfish decision.

I hopped and skipped along the way,
There was no more time for delay.
Struck by a feeling of urgency,
A telepathic message transmitted emergency.

The menacing bird said,
"Kiskadee, Kiskadee, your mother's dead."
This strange refrain stuck in my head.
What could I do in such a nervous state
But to hope and pray I would not be late.

I entered the hospital speedily
Remembering what the Kiskadee had sung eerily.
I rushed to her already-empty bed
And knew for sure my mother was dead.

I bowed my head and began to cry,
'Dear God, why did my mother have to die?"
Cricket had robbed me of seeing my mother,
And now I was alone without even a brother.

Aunt Madeline

Aunt Madeline,
An excellent cook,
Lived to a hundred and seven.
I'm sure she's in heaven,
Thank God for her life.

She shone in the kitchen
Making many a dish
Tasty fish,
Finger-licking baked chicken
Cow-heel soup,
Rice and peas,
All made to please.

A wonderful old lady
Immaculately dressed,
Her white cap and apron
All fresh.
Thank God for her example.

Although her English
Was not up to par,
All who visited the vicarage
Loved this old star.
If you ate her meals
You were truly blessed.
Thankfully, I confess.

Youth

O Youth, is there no end to your scorn?
Your macabre humor mocks the human race
Who finds it difficult to keep pace
With age, the dreaded foe, who smiles at us each morn.

You remain illusive and aloof
While humans try to capture your worth
Claiming it was a gift from birth
Yet desperately searching for reaffirming proof.

The world awaits a jubilant day
When we our youth will regain.
But more importantly to be able to maintain
Youth, which will constantly be on display.

Bullying

Bullying at school is nothing new.
Believe it or not, I suffered too.
Of course, this does not make it right
All such evils should be brought to light.

How I hated having to go to school.
The culprits, on the other hand, thought it was cool
To push and punch an innocent person,
Bragging about teaching me a lesson.

Often, parents and teachers do not know
Because the lumps and bruises do not show.
Yet the victim suffers excruciating pain
And wishes it never happens again.

Be vigilant and helpful all who hear
Because no one should experience such fear.
Try to do whatever it takes
To correct these dreadful mistakes.

Hummingbird

Haven't you heard?
I belong to the smallest species of bird.
Does this sound absurd?
I am a hummingbird.

I am known for my rapid flight,
And much to my delight,
The beat of my strong wings produce a hum
Which sounds like a miniature drum.

Nectar, the food of the gods, is my sustenance.
Extracting it from flowers offer no resistance.
My ability to fly backward is truly a steal
Such euphoria other birds will never feel.

My opalescent plumage is basically metallic green
While my throat displays colors rarely seen.
A necklace of glittering red, emerald green and blue
Baffle admirers when they discover it's really true.

Three hundred species show my pedigree
A royal heritage for all to see.
The Americas have always been home to us
But South America is preferred from dawn to dusk.

The Peacock

Exotic feathers of rare design
Stir the imagination of the mind.
The peacock is a unique bird
That is truly a gift from the Lord.

His outstanding and magnificent display
Is a source of pride he exhibits each day.
The peacock, who certainly knows what to wear,
Uses his plumage to enhance his rear.

His coat of iridescent green and gold
Has fetched a tidy sum when sold
All because of an eye-like quilt on electric blue
Which gives the appearance of a fascinating hue.

The peacock, who puffs and struts his stuff,
Knows his beauty is more than good enough,
So he always walks with his head in the cloud.
Surely, he has a valid reason to be proud.

Journey of Discovery

Thunder, Lightning and Rain

Thunder, lightning and rain
Displace many individuals and cause much pain,
These offsprings of nature
Force us to look at the bigger picture.

The clap of thunder, a deafening sound,
Awakens and alerts folks for miles around.
These elements, which are not always kind,
Are known to drive individuals out of their mind.

The flashes of lightning,
Which are usually frightening,
Emerge as a precursor to inclement weather
And ofttimes cause individuals to huddle together.

Then comes the downpours of showers of rain
With a noisy clatter on the windowpane.
Everyone in sight quickly runs for cover
While domestic partners cuddle their lover.

The witches in *Macbeth* hoped to meet again
Maybe in thunder, lightning or in rain.
This Shakespearean reminder underscores the fact
That the assault of these elements causes us all to react.

The Mind and Spirit Embrace Each Other

Journey of Discovery

I Dreamt I Went to Heaven

I dreamt I went to heaven
And saw the Promised Land
It was a mere glimpse given
To someone who could understand.

Was this some kind of confusion
Lurking in my head
Or did I receive a contusion
As I lay upon my bed.

I visited an unusual garden
Where I could not believe my eyes.
The trees with leaves of gold were laden
With diamonds, garnets, crystals
and emeralds of every size.

The ground no less shimmered in a different light
With quarters, nickels and dimes.
The reflection of jewels and coins
almost blinded my sight
When suddenly I heard the peal of heavenly
chimes.

One moment in time would be too much to delay
So I jumped up at the sound of my alarm clock
Waking me up to welcome a newborn day.
Opening my eyes, I instantly knew that all along I
had been in shock.

The Rose

Poets, painters and amateurs
Down the ages spread the good news
Of your fragrance, color and beauty
Which attract us out of duty.

Your colors of hue
Are too good to be true.
Velvety petals caress the morning dew
While neighboring flowers smile back at you.

Yet clothing of thorns you wear,
As if to shield yourself from fear,
Or is it the legend of humanity's fall?
A sad reminder to us all.

Treasure Chests

I opened my back door
And lo, what did I behold?
Dewdrops sitting on blades of green grass
A fascinating sight I could not bypass.

Patterns of diamonds everywhere
seem to welcome the sun,
Informing me that observing nature
really can be fun.
Daily we past treasure chests of great worth
Simply because we lack the discerning eyes
of William Wordsworth.

The Cross on the Wall

I hang upon a simple wall
Clothed in silver beads and mother-of-pearl.
The red color that you see
Is not blood as appears to be.

Red roses peep out from under my arm
So there is no cause for alarm.
Can you understand my state?
I am a symbol of true faith.

A cross is what should come to mind
Because I am one of a kind.
The morning sun shines on my face
Making a pattern that interlace.

I am indeed a work of art
So let my presence touch your heart
And as you begin to pray
Think of Christ's life from day to day.

Journey of Discovery

God Strengthens Marriage

Ten years have come and gone
Since you your vows have made
No longer do you seen forlorn
Knowing true love will never fade.

Almighty God had bound you together
As an example for others to see
That patience, kindness and understanding
are forever
Regardless of what others may think them to be.

Your Heavenly Father is your rock
So trust Him with all your heart.
Remember as members of His flock
He blessed you from the start.

Dedicated to Christopher and Sandra Hunte

Nine-Eleven

These numbers will always be talked about.
On nine-eleven two thousand and one,
Eye witnesses began to shout
When calamity struck and left us all forlorn.

A painful day to remember,
We saw Manhattan being attacked from the start.
It occurred in the month of September.
Lives of families were instantly torn apart.

The Twin Towers, a picturesque site,
Were targeted by planes on that fatal morning.
Architectural fixtures were removed from sight.
Soon, relatives of trapped victims were in mourning.

Pandemonium broke out in our great city
As billows of smoke, soot and scattered litter
Covered everything and everyone in a jiffy.
This made observers horrified and bitter.

This example of mankind's anger
Will be recorded in history as a day of carnage.
Impending doom will hover forever
As a gruesome reminder of this sinister age.

A Mother's Prayer

Sincere good wishes to my firstborn,
How welcome was that glorious morn.
When you uttered your first cry
It sounded like an angel's sigh.

You have been such a blessing to me
Sharing our love and joy for all to see.
No one can ever keep us apart
Even when from this life we both depart.

You, my daughter, are a beacon of light
And have always sought to do what is right.
Your deep concern for others is a trait
That has shown your immense faith.

Mothers assuredly understand
God has everything in His hand.
May love and peace be yours forever
As the Omnipotent blesses your endeavor.

God Answers Prayers

The day you answered the Master's call
God entrusted you to us all.
Your patience, guidance and love
Are truly blessings from above.

These past years you have shown true commitment
And now God has granted you a measure of fulfillment.
Friends who helped you along the way
Treasure your friendship more than words can say.

We know that God answers prayer
So we asked him to keep you in His care
As friends, this is the best we can do
Simply because we love and cherish you.

Dedicated to Rev. Canon Howard K. Williams from your friends Christopher & Sandra Hunte with much love and prayers.

Preachers Are Humans

What is it some preachers have in common?
They love to drink and play backgammon.
Alcohol has become the beverage of the day
Regardless what folks may think or say.

But who are we to ridicule?
God knows how and when to rule.
The day of accountability will appear
So trust in the Lord and do not despair.

Think of your own abomination,
And as Paul advised, work out your salvation.
Do not take others' weaknesses to heart,
Simply live your life and do your part.

Who knows how hard folks may try
Just to serve the Lord and remain dry.
Of course, you can help by offering up a prayer
To God Almighty who is ready to hear.

Preachers are humans just as we are
Although at times they seem so far.
Continue to worship and do your best
And remember you too will be put to the test.

A Chosen Vessel

Today is the beginning of another milestone in your life.
God elevated you above anger and strife.
The order of MELCHIZEDEK to which you belong,
Is a daily reminder, "In God be strong."

Continue to be a healer in every circumstance.
In fact, treat every situation as a godly romance.
To whom much is given much is expected.
Remember the Son of God was himself rejected.

Your mother smiles and blesses you today
As she looks down from heaven upon this grand display.
Your father still lives to tell the tale,
Trust in God and you will never fail.

May God continue to bless your future years.
Be not discouraged and entertain no fears.
Remember humility is the key.
You are chosen vessel for all to see.

God's richest blessings to Rev. Canon Howard K. Williams, now and always.

Lloyd & Michelle Andries

ASSESSING LIFE

Journey of Discovery

Diamonds Are Forever

Like a diamond, you have shone through the years,
Notwithstanding fear, pain or tears.
Fate at times has been unkind
But you weathered the storm because of your mind.

Prayer, love and patience too
Revealed the wealth of strength in you.
Mortals such as we are
Need the guidance of a star.

You allowed the Almighty to do just this.
Henceforth, there can be nothing but bliss.
Winter, Autumn, Summer, Spring may bring.
A little of this, a little of that, a little of everything.

Unmoved by it all may you continue to be
The loving person we now see.
Diamonds are forever and so can you
If to yourself you remain true.

Sixty years are a mere revelation
Of someone growing in faith and embracing salvation.
So continue to live and experience life my friend
Because this is what really matters in the end.

A Happy Occasion

A birthday is a happy occasion
And has been from generation to generation.
Yet, accolades and gifts are more meaningful
If at seventy-five you are still beautiful.

You have acquired many attributes through the years
Even though you experienced blood, sweat and tears.
Your tenacity has been a rule of thumb,
Showing your critics that you are not dumb.
The road at times has been rough
But you hung in there and remained tough.
No one should begrudge you your right
As a person of fortitude and light.

Your children are no less to be praised
For the way in which they were raised.
Your Christian values were always strong
Teaching them right from wrong.

So may this day be remembered by them
And praise God with a loud Amen.
For He has been your constant guide
Elevating this family to a place of pride.

Dedicated to Antoinetta Jordan

Beautiful Memories

Decades ago, you bade us goodbye
In your usual quiet way.
It broke our hearts then made us cry
But your presence did with us stay.

Your beautiful face and Mona Lisa smile
Gave many people pleasure.
Your long hair and gorgeous figure
no less did beguile
Such beautiful memories of you we still treasure.

Photographs of you on display
Are placed in prominent places.
It never ceases to brighten our day
As you light up visitors' faces.

As husband and daughter we recall your beauty
Including your outstanding gifts as a nurse, too
You exemplified dedication to duty
In whatever you had to do.

We will continue to cherish your memory
No matter what the future brings
Because your life has been a testimony
Filled with love and many good things.

In loving memory of Barbara Taljit Andries
From The Rev. Dr. Lloyd Andries
& daughter Michelle Andries

Hasta Luego

You have been a loving and faithful husband throughout the years.
The time has come to say farewell and all I have to offer you are tears.
But no outward expression can alleviate the pain
Because death is a sad reminder of a solemn refrain.

We did so many things together and had such fun
Now your earthly task is finished, God's will be done.
Memories of words and deeds will ever with me stay
And I thank God for the precious gifts given to me each day.

Goodbye sounds too final to come from my mouth
Knowing I will see you again without a doubt.
Hasta Luego to the love of my life,
I will forever be grateful you made me your wife.

You have answered God's call to a better place
And now I await that moment when I shall gaze upon your face.
Until such time, I will continue to cherish our love
Because it was a special gift from heaven above.

Death Be Not Unkind

The pain of death is very real
For those who experience loss
It is something only they can feel
As they struggle to bear a heavy cross.

Friends often join the mourners,
And their concern is of the very best,
But it is not an easy time for even bystanders
When a loved one is being laid to rest.

No preparation can prepare you for the hurt
When sad news would disturb your mind
And the surge of pent-up emotions evoke outburst,
"O Death, how could you be so unkind?"

In memory of James Harry Massiah, my high school friend and buddy.

Living and Loving

Yankees Collapse

The theme, "Take me out to the ball game"
May well be sung with a different refrain,
"Take me out of Yankee Stadium the recent Hall of Shame
Where New York fans hoped that it would rain."

For years, the Yankees ball club seemed almost invincible,
But fame is as cunning as an old fox.
We were about to witness the inconceivable
As Boston fans cheered on the Red Sox.

The Red Sox enjoyed the feeling of jubilation
When they sensed the Yankees collapse would occur at home.
This was their moment of salvation,
Alas! Failure was not destined for them alone.

It is said, "All is fair in love and war."
Sports allow an equal opportunity for all.
New York fans will continue to support their star,
Convinced that sooner or later the Red Sox will fall.

The Dentist's Chair

Fifteenth June two thousand and four
Was certainly a memorable day.
My dental appointment on the twenty-ninth floor
Made me take the elevator without delay.

Upon entering the air-conditioned room,
The receptionist flashed a Colgate smile
Appropriately directed to someone downcast with gloom
Because my dental records were here on file.

The time had come to sit in The Dentist's Chair,
Giving me a brief moment to enjoy a panoramic view
Which certainly helped to allay my fear.
Honestly, this picture would soothe even a weeping child of two.

"Open your mouth," was a gentle reminder
A brilliant overhead light exposed eroding gum and cavitied teeth.
My dentist, with dexterity and skill, began by using a sonic scaler.
Suction pump, noisy drill all directed a thrill to my sensitive feet.

Journey of Discovery

Today was special because I had to wear a crown.
At last, my mouth would look complete and neat.
The adjusting and fixing were easily done
So now I can smile openly and show my teeth.

A precautionary thought jogged my brain,
From now on pay strict attention to dental care.
Thankfully, anesthesia eased my pain
But I was more than eager to step out of The
Dentist's Chair.

Fashion

I was born in the Garden of Eden
My parents are Adam and Eve
From the moment they donned fig leaves
I was unknowingly conceived
My name is Fashion.

I live in many countries of the world
And speak different languages.
Race, color and even ethnicity are appropriate
Because originality is my motto.
I am Fashion.

Designers who dare to show off sartorial skill
Copy my unique style.
My first display was breathtaking and eye-popping
When Adam saw Eve wearing a leaf and a smile.
This was the birth of Fashion.

Today's runaways have many alluring models
Who strut and twist to show the stuff
Of which designers are made.
A spool of determination, a thimble of genius and a needling desire
To make Fashion.

The Adorable Diva

The years have given us much to remember.
How well I recall that cold mid-December
When I attended a special Christmas concert
And heard a celestial voice right here on earth.

The Adorable Diva appeared on the scene
Wearing an emerald green gown fit for a Queen.
Her angelic voice flooded the building with a melodious sound
That made her the rave of all around.

Her interpretation and artistry are unique,
Matched only by her outstanding beauty and physique.
She caresses and soothes your nerves
Using her remarkable gift as one who serves.

Whenever the occasion arises for a dramatic aria,
Then we truly experience the power of the full-throated diva.
Her voice will continue to give immeasurable pleasure
Because she is truly a God-given treasure.

Enduring Beauty

From the moment of your birth,
Folks around you were filled with mirth.
You began to kick and scream
So they named you Norma Jeane.

Your craving for attention began to show
Long before you were known as Marilyn Monroe.
Even Venus, the goddess of love,
Could not dethrone one chosen from above.

Your hair, face and figure declared war
On photographers who dared to snap a rare star.
Your enduring beauty and sex appeal
Many admirers would try to steal.

But no one could really imitate
A vision of beauty destined for an unusual fate.
Your face and name will ever be seen
As your movies replay on the silver screen.

You have now become a legend by name
Because you captured illusive fame.
Celebrities worship at your shrine
Hoping you could teach them how to shine.

Your insatiable thirst for knowledge seemed so right
When you married Arthur Miller, the renowned playwright.
However, nothing was written in stone
So once you divorced him you were left alone.

Journey of Discovery

The paparazzi and tabloids had a field day
When your pose for "The Seven-Year Itch" made grand display.
Your then-husband, Joe DiMaggio, of baseball fame,
Felt he could no longer endure such shame.

Leaving you was the straw that broke the camel's back.
You sought refuge in depression and the sack.
Admired by millions, even a president,
You would soon find solace in cold cement.

Gone but never to be forgotten by generations to come.
You will always remain famous to many if not some.
Goddesses of all sorts may come and go
But none will erupt as pleasurable memories as Marilyn Monroe.

A Love That Dares Not Whisper Its Name

There's a love not unheard of
Yet it's a love that dares not whisper its name.
Counts and monks, kings and queens, celibates and reprobates
Have all enjoyed its nectar
While unknowingly they worship the goddess Ishtar.

Famous persons like Lawrence of Arabia and the Queen of Sheba
Swallowed their pride and rather than hide
Succumbed to a love that dares not whisper its name.
The euphoria and plethora will only be known
By those who enjoy the satisfaction to reap what they have sown.

Journey of Discovery

A World Awaits Your Skill

It seems as only yesterday
An act of love was on display,
A beautiful baby girl was born
A welcome gift on a glorious morn.

Your nurturing parents watched you grow
Their searching eyes always aglow.
As each day brought a sense of satisfaction
Knowing their pride and joy was such an attraction.

Not many years have passed
And now their daughter has amassed.
A Bachelor's of Art and a Master's degree,
Proving her worth and pedigree.

Time and knowledge have embraced Fate
And now you are about to graduate.
Move boldly into a world that awaits your skill.
Share your talents and your dreams fulfill.

Dedicated to my god daughter, Carol Guthrie

A Time of Maturation

Congratulations to my god daughter.
You can once again display mirth and laughter.
At times, studying seemed such a bore
But it was a relief from many a household chore.

You showed remarkable patience and dedication,
Earning yourself a Bachelor's of Arts and a Master's in Education
While this is the day for your graduation
It is also a time of maturation.

You will now join a world full of romantics,
But you will become a teacher of mathematics
Family and friends are proud of your achievement.
This accomplishment should bring you great contentment.

May God continue to bless you
As you follow Him and to yourself remain true.
Temptations will always hover in the air
But with God as your guide you need not fear.

ENVISIONING HOPE

Journey of Discovery

Tsunami

Tsunami fear
Waters dare
Tsunami scare
Lands now bare

Tsunami scare
Waters dare
Houses tumble
People fumble

Tsunami fear
Tsunami scare
Waters everywhere
No time to stare

Tsunami dare
Erupts fear
Innocent people
Instantly feeble

Tsunami scare
Tsunami fear
Tsunami sounds
Like gigantic drums

Tsunami fear
Waters dare
Tsunami scare
Lands now bare.

Arise, Grenada

Grenada, colorful Isle of Spice
So often have I walked upon the beautiful Grand Anse beach,
To me the island's picturesque sceneries were ever so nice.
Now all of this is certainly out of reach.

Hurricane Ivan created such wanton destruction
That even your dormant ancestors were aroused from their sleep.
The powerful winds and torrential rains caused utter devastation.
Many lives were lost and those alive could only weep.

You are a country whose people have experienced disaster before
But you are resilient and can reclaim your former glory.
Your people's strength and deep faith are still in store.
So rise up from the ashes and write a new chapter in history.

Bury Nature's wrath as you did in the past.
Use courage and hard work to achieve your aim
Then the world will truly believe Grenada can and will last
Because you did not allow circumstance to enjoy its shame.

Gird up your loins and put your people to the test.
In rebuilding, let your faith and tenacity encourage you.
Shake off the shackles of the recent mess
And show the world what Grenadians can do.

The Ultimate Blessing

When I consider my good fortune
I marvel how blessed I've been.
My body has always been in tune
But now things are not what they seem.

I know that God will strengthen me
Especially in this time of need.
His love and constant care will forever be
The source of strength on which I feed.
I give thanks for friends so kind and true
And for the patience and understanding shown by all.
This is a hallmark of dedication and definitely a clue
That angels surround us daily and await our call.

This disease named cancer is a killer to be sure.
It ravages the body through and through.
Hopefully, science will some day discover a cure.
Until that time, there's not much one can do.

If at times I seem ungrateful and difficult to please
Do not judge me harshly just pray for me to grow in grace
And to believe that one day all my pains will ease,
Then I shall enjoy the ultimate blessing of meeting God
Face to Face.

Dedicated to all cancer patients

Cold and Exposed

Standing tall and upright,
My leaves once green now turn russet, orange, gold.
The howling winds shake my limbs from le ft to right
And I tremble while being undressed in the cold.

One by one my colorful leaves fall to the ground
During this season I am usually stripped bare.
My discarded foliage is all around
Forming nature's carpets, a compelling reason to stare.

Now I stand cold and exposed,
A mere shadow of my former self.
Some would accuse the ruthless winds for my woes
But I have no one to blame but myself.

I am a tree for all seasons
So why should I complain about the lack of fun
Even though I could give many reasons
To avoid the cold and bask in the sun.

Good Friday

Alas! This was a dreadful day.
Yet, surprisingly, it is called Good Friday.
It proved to be quite a paradox,
Having been engineered by Pilate that cunning fox.

Alas! A man who had done so much good
Should be crucified upon a cross of wood.
He lived a life unblemished in deed
And because of this He was able to succeed.

This angered the authorities at large
Who sought an opportunity to discharge
Accusations of all sorts of behavior
Which led to the condemnation of our Savior.

Trials, mockeries, scourgings and beatings
Followed a series of impromptu meetings.
But this is how it was foretold to be
That someone should die for you and me.

This was an immense sacrifice for sure
Considering the brutality He had to endure
Yet His Father's will had to be done
And this involved all and not just some.

On The Via Dolorosa to Mount Calvary
He carried his own cross for all to see.
The authorities thought that they had won,
And during that moment they had great fun.

Journey of Discovery

The Good Friday crucifixion was an awful scene
Which showed how mankind can be so mean.
This moment in history was not the end
As we now know the Resurrection was just around the bend.

Brooklyn

Brooklyn, borough of promise and pure delight,
You stir up pleasant memories of long ago.
Now residents with keen foresight
Will rekindle that special spark and glow.

Your sons and daughters have made their mark
From New York to California and beyond.
Indeed, your offsprings are very smart
To promote your name and forge a lasting bond.

Artists, athletes, politicians, educators and entrepreneurs
Will forever extol their place of birth
Because they are in no way amateurs
But professionals who have proven their worth.

Thanksgiving and praise for Brooklyn once more,
A borough destined for perpetual fame.
Visitors will soon come to tour
A unique place with a well-known name.

Journey of Discovery

The Saffron Gates of Central Park

Twenty-five years in the making,
This was indeed heartbreaking
But Christo and his partner Jeanne Claude
Eventually were able to unveil their fad.

Spectators arrived by millions to see
A costly experience of Art that was free
The choreographed movements of the cloth
Gave an illusion of colors – orange, tan and gold of great worth.

The trees and skyline formed a magnificent backdrop
As the breeze swayed each saffron gate held up at the top.
Seventy-five hundred of sixteen-foot-tall fabric gates
Danced and waved at passersby, many with their mates.

To the creative eye, this was certainly a treat.
The skeptics saw it as a lot of fuss and a cheat.
No one knows how long these impressions will last
But for certain, "The Gates" are now a thing of the past.

Image

Image is such an adorable thing
Yet distorted as can be
Because individuals only bring
The portrait they want you to see.

This image projected is ofttimes false,
And because people are gullible
They are taken for a waltz
By someone who is downright unreliable.

However, expectations continue to be high
By people without a clue
Who see you as a lovable guy
And the champion of a crew.

Journey of Discovery

A Second Chance

The news broadcast on that fatal morning
Shocked the basketball world and fans of Alonzo Mourning.
He was diagnosed with Focal Segmental Glomenulosclerosis.
But there was hope once a suitable donor was found to assist.

Dr. Appel, Director of Nephrology at Columbia University Medical Center,
Soon became 'Zo's' close friend and mentor.
He cautioned that the danger could not be overstated.
In the meanwhile, Mourning's kidney deteriorated.

At last! a relative and matching donor was found.
Jason Cooper's kind gesture and tests proved to be sound.
The National Basketball Association All-Star would be given a second chance
To prove that his ability was not due to happenstance.

The kidney transplant was a huge success.
Thank God for alleviating his pain and distress.
Alonzo will continue to praise God's name.
Living a life worthy of Him through Basketball fame.

An Old Woman of East Indian Birth

Now I am old and can hardly see
To make my mouthwatering jalebi
But I can still make dhal and mango chutney.
And people love my roti and curry.

All my children have families of their own,
And I have grandchildren who are full grown
Many of whom are doctors and lawyers in foreign lands.
I pray to God daily to keep them safe in His hands.

Enduring the hot sun while planting in the rice field
Is now the product of a wonderful family yield.
Feeding the animals and milking the cow
Was worth the sweat and wiping of my brow.

An Old Woman of East Indian birth
Is living proof of what hard work is worth.
Now that I can hardly see daylight,
I thank God for giving me foresight.

Journey of Discovery

I Remember You, Ma

Now that you have gone
I feel lost and forlorn.
The days of yore
Were never a bore.

I remember you, Ma
From the time I could utter ta-ta.
The time when I held on to your skirt
My bottle in my mouth, what a little flirt.

You always made me feel secure
Regardless of what I had to endure.
You knew exactly what to say
Using words that would melt even clay.

Your death was indeed a sad farewell.
You are no longer here for me to tell
My burning hopes and hidden fears.
Even when I feel the flow of warm tears.

I remember you, Ma
But the time has come to say ta-ta.
In my heart you will always be around
Because your love has been very profound.

In memory of Latchmin Sumintra Bridgelall

God Will Provide

Can we really trust the Lord?
Of course, He always keeps his Word.
He is, after all, the Almighty
Who encouraged the lame to walk and made the
blind to see.

Can we really believe in Him?
Why, certainly, because He was without sin.
Think of Him as The Transcendent and
Omnipotent One
Who even takes care of the unborn.

God is Omniscient and full of wisdom.
Through faith, we can enter into His kingdom.
Simply trust and believe in His bounty
And we shall share in His Horn of Plenty.

Why bother about finding a solution
When God is our ultimate salvation.
He will never leave us penniless.
As His children we are greatly blessed.

Yes, God will provide for us all
As He did even before the Fall.
He gives to us our daily bread,
Making sure we are always fed.